THE CAREGIVER'S BOOK

Caring for Another, Caring for Yourself

P9-CSV-948

TEXT AND PHOTOGRAPHY
BY JAMES E. MILLER

Augsburg
MINNEAPOLIS

To my sister, Patty Lee, with love.

ACKNOWLEDGMENTS

Several people helped in the development of ideas for this book. Connie Croyle, Kay Roberts, Roxandra Clemmons-McFarthing, Clare Barton, Jennifer Levine, John Peterson, Bernie Miller, and Ron Williams each added thoughts and insights. Jennifer Levine and Patty Lee generously shared their ideas for the Suggestions pages. Bob Klausmeier edited this book, his third for me, with an accuracy and sensitivity that I have come to respect and admire. This book is, in every way, a collaboration.

THE CAREGIVER'S BOOK
Caring for Another, Caring for Yourself

Copyright © 1996 Augsburg Fortress. All rights reserved. Except for brief quotations in critical articles or reviews, no part of this book may be reproduced in any manner without prior written permission from the publisher. Write to: Permissions, Augsburg Fortress, 426 S. Fifth St., Box 1209, Minneapolis, MN 55440.

The paper used in this publication meets the minimum requirements of American National Standard for Information Sciences—Permanence of Paper for Printed Library Materials, ANSI Z329.48-1984.   ∞

Manufactured in the U.S.A.   AF 9-2985

00   99   2   3   4   5   6   7   8   9   10

Library of Congress Cataloging-in-Publication Data and other copyright information will be found at the end of this book.

FOREWORD

Caregiving. The word brings to mind beautiful images of compassion and self-sacrifice: cradling a newborn baby, comforting a person who is ill or dying, supporting someone who is bereaved. Healthy caregiving can bring out all that is best in us. And that *is* beautiful.

But there is another side to caregiving—a side we may not care to think about or talk about. Done without adequate rest or relief, caregiving becomes a chore and a drain. Done without proper knowledge and support, it becomes confusing and harrowing. Done without appreciation or understanding, it turns disappointing or disheartening.

You will be confronted with this other side of caregiving, whether you're a trained professional or a volunteer caring for family members or friends. If you're like most people, you weren't prepared for all the demands required by ongoing caregiving. If you're like me, you went into the experience filled with high hopes and good intentions, and then discovered you lacked something—something critical.

I've written this book for caregivers like you. These pages hold images from many people's lives, including my own. Perhaps you'll find your own life pictured here as well. I hope you'll take your time as you read the book. Reflect on the quotations and photographs. Try out the suggestions. Mostly, let the pages help you step back to get a clearer, more accurate picture of your caregiving, to see in it an adventure you'll not soon forget and a privilege you'll always cherish.

Fort Wayne, Indiana

Since you've chosen this book,

or someone has chosen it for you,

chances are you're a caregiver, or are about to become one.

Either way, you know that caregiving is a sobering task.

Becoming responsible for another's care takes courage as well as energy,

firmness as well as tenderness,

self-discipline as well as self-sacrifice.

It can be a terribly demanding role.

It is also a terribly important role.

Another's well-being may depend upon what you do.

The one in your care may rely upon you for daily sustenance,

physical comfort, a dose of encouragement.

You may be called upon to perform specialized procedures,

to collaborate with medical personnel,

and a host of other duties.

If you're caring for a family member or friend,

you probably have many other responsibilities in your life as well,

and perhaps many other worries.

If you're a professional caregiver,

you may also face pressures of patient loads, paperwork, and staff relationships,

in addition to your own challenges in life.

To compound the situation, some of you may have no training or experience in providing such personal attention for another human being.

Where is empathy taught?

Who is the instructor for setting boundaries?

How do you learn to listen well?

All questions like these point eventually to one question:

How do you provide care that is healthy—

healthy for the other, and for yourself at the same time?

This book attempts to provide ideas about wise caregiving.

It's designed to meet the needs of those who are busy with chores,

those who are perhaps strained with responsibilities.

Eight general ideas will be presented, with specific suggestions under each.

There will also be photos for you to explore,

and wisdom from the ages for you to fathom.

Words will be kept to a minimum,

so your thoughts and feelings will have plenty of room to roam.

As you will see by making your way through these pages,

caregiving is not all duty and demands.

Caregiving also can be a wonderful adventure,

a marvelous privilege, and an unspeakable grace.

If you have not discovered that already, you will.

The healthiest way to care for another is to care for yourself.

If you're like most caregivers,

    the needs of the person entrusted to your care are very important to you.

If they're ill or in pain, if they're frightened or upset,

    you want to ease their discomfort, to soothe their feelings.

If they're facing long-term limitations or long-suffering decline,

    you want to provide supportive assistance,

        in the way they desire.

You are in a position to make a real difference in their life.

You can be mature enough to put their interests ahead of your own.

You can be gracious enough to help them even when you're tired,

    to encourage them even when you feel low,

        to pamper them even when you'd like to be pampered yourself.

But, without being aware of what you're doing, and for the best of reasons,

    you can also endanger your caregiving.

When caring for another becomes a significant part of how you spend your days,
then caring for yourself becomes equally important.

In order to give, you must have something within you to give.

In order to share your strength, you must have ways to marshal that strength.

In order to offer something fresh to that person who needs it,
you must find ways to be refreshed yourself.

Caring for yourself is not a matter of selfishness or unselfishness.

It's a matter of keeping yourself replenished and healthy
so you can give your most beneficial and wholesome care.

No matter how encompassing the other person's needs,
you have needs that are no less important.

For your sake, and for the other person's sake,
your needs as a human being deserve consideration too.

Begin by becoming aware of your personal needs,
     just as you're aware of the needs of the one you're caring for.
Then work to satisfy those.
Find ways to get the rest you cannot do without,
     however strong you are, however loving you feel.
Maintain your energy by eating healthily and drinking wisely.
Build your stamina by exercising regularly.
Make sure you set aside time each day just for yourself.
Open yourself to healing influences all around you—
     through prayer and meditation, in nature, art, music, literature.
Allow yourself opportunities for fun.
Indulge yourself from time to time.
Engage in those practices that expand your mind and touch your soul.
Remember: *only* by caring for yourself can you adequately care for another.

Love is not a possession but a growth.
The heart is a lamp with just enough oil to burn for an hour,
and if there be no oil to put in again, its light will go out.
God's peace is the oil that fills the lamp of love.

HENRY WARD BEECHER

Help thyself, and God will help thee.

GEORGE HERBERT

I am only one,
But still I am one.
I cannot do everything,
But still I can do something.
And because I cannot do everything
I will not refuse to do the something that I can do.

EDWARD EVERETT HALE

For the whole law is summed up in a single commandment,
"You shall love your neighbor as yourself."

GALATIANS 5:14

SUGGESTIONS

List things you can do to care for yourself.
For example: "Take a long hot bath." "Order out Chinese food." "Read the latest mystery novel." Make a long list of favorite activities that help restore you. Go over your list to see how regularly you do these things. Put the list where you'll see it—like on your refrigerator—and make a check mark beside an item each time you do it. If you're not making several check marks a day, recall how important it is to take care of yourself. Then start doing more for yourself that very day.

Develop a plan for respite care.
Figure out ways to provide for the one in your care while you get away for short breaks. Schedule those breaks in advance. When someone says, "Let me know if I can do anything to help," take them up on the offer. Do you have family members or friends or neighbors who could help you? When? How? How about members of your congregation? Does a day-care center provide services in your community? Are home-care services available on a part-time basis? Check out all options—and then make use of them. Every once in a while, plan a longer period away so you can really refresh yourself. Try always to know when your next break will be, so you've got something to look forward to.

Celebrate "unbirthdays."
For no reason at all, and for the best of reasons, throw an all-day "unbirthday" party now and again. Do it for yourself, do it for the person in your care, and do it for both of you together. Put up decorations. Wrap little gifts. Arrange a bouquet of flowers. Wear party clothes. Eat a special meal. Play favorite music. And have an "unbirthday" cake, of course—one that can hold all the candles you want to add. Whoop it up. Go to bed at night with a smile on your face.

By focusing on your feelings, you can focus *beyond* your feelings.

You may have thought that, as a caregiver,

    you're always supposed to rise above your feelings.

You may believe you're supposed to do whatever is required of you

    without letting your emotions get involved.

That expectation is unfair and unhealthy,

    for genuine caregiving involves your whole self—including your emotions.

Caregiving naturally activates so much inside you:

    concern for what's happening to the person you care for;

        feelings about that person as a human being;

            reactions to the tasks that are yours to perform;

                responses to others with whom you interact;

                anticipation about what lies ahead.

Your feelings can help you get a clearer sense

    of what's going on all around you.

So don't hide your feelings or ignore them; value them.

A cardinal rule for caregivers is this:
feel whatever it is you feel, and feel it as fully as you can.

The range of feelings you may experience is vast.

You may fear you cannot do all it appears you must do.

At times you may feel more tired than you'd wish,
more anxious than you'd like to admit,
more saddened than you'd want to express.

You may feel frustrated for any number of reasons—
or resentful, or bitter, or even furious.

You may feel sorry for yourself, or for the one in your care,
or for both of you together.

Then again, you may feel pleased you're able to do what you can.

You may be proud of what you're accomplishing together.

You may be grateful for blessings both large and small.

You may feel great love.

Remember that all your feelings are valid,

all are worth your attention and your expression.

For in the act of drawing out what is inside yourself,

wonderful things can happen.

You can learn and grow.

You can become more free, more sure, more whole.

So find someone you can talk to and give your feelings a voice.

But be open to releasing your feelings in other ways, too.

You may cry them, or laugh them, or paint them.

You may write them, or sing them, or pray them.

Don't be surprised if the feelings conflict with one another.

That's not unusual when so much is going on inside and outside of you.

By focusing on your emotions,

and by freeing them in ways best suited to you,

you can help ensure your feelings do not get in the way of your caregiving.

*Never apologize for showing feeling.
When you do so, you apologize for truth.*
BENJAMIN DISRAELI

*It is not a matter of thinking a great deal
but of loving a great deal,
so do whatever arouses you most to love.*
TERESA OF AVILA

*Respect in yourself the oscillations of feelings:
they are your life and your nature;
a wiser than you made them.*
HENRI AMIEL

*There is no feeling in a human heart that exists in that heart
alone—which is not, in some form or degree, in every heart.*
GEORGE MACDONALD

SUGGESTIONS

Find someone whom you can honestly share your feelings with.
Every caregiver deserves the opportunity to open up to another human being, knowing that what they say will be accepted, respected, and kept in confidence. Speaking your feelings to another is a way of unbottling them, a way to help you stay healthy. You can also get a better perspective on your role—what you like and dislike about it. You can learn more about your emotions, too—how and why they change, how they can be useful, how they can be both predictable and surprising. Just make sure the listener is not the one you're caring for; you need someone more objective.

Journal.
Write about what's going on in your life, especially what's going on inside you. Write about your feelings, insights, reflections. Try doing this once a day, or at least several times a week. Find a comfortable place where you can have quiet and privacy. Write in a notebook if you prefer, or tap away on a computer keyboard. Let your thoughts and feelings flow, and put down whatever surfaces. Every so often, read back over your entries. Ask yourself, "What am I learning? How am I growing?"

Let off steam physically.
Even if your caregiving involves lots of physical exercise, it helps to set aside time for special activities that honor your body and help clear your mind. What works for you? Aerobics or swimming? Yoga or tai chi? Jogging? Long, brisk, or leisurely walks? Some people like to vacuum with a vengeance. Others enjoy group sports or working in the garden. Keeping your body in shape is a good way to help keep your mind in shape. You'll be a better person and a better caregiver for it.

To be close, you must establish boundaries.

When the needs of someone you care for are great,

    or when you have become part of the other's life in so many ways,

        you may desire to draw as close as possible.

You may be inclined to keep that person always at the forefront of your thoughts.

You may try to keep yourself always within easy reach of their grasp.

You may find yourself almost merging with the other person,

    so whatever happens to them happens to you.

Whatever they feel, you feel.

Whatever upsets them, upsets you.

Whatever their pain, you take it on as your own.

Identifying so completely with another

    is an ideal some caregivers have sought.

But it is less than ideal.

To be a good caregiver, you must maintain your separateness.
   While you may care deeply for that other person,
      you are still your own unique self.
You have your own life to claim.
And that includes having your own limits to set.
There are times when it's appropriate to say "no,"
   however much your care, and even *because* you care.
There are times when it makes sense to guard your privacy,
   to protect your creativity, to preserve your other relationships.
There are times when it's natural to give yourself a reprieve from your work
   by asking another to help you, or to be there in your place.
In recognizing that sometimes you may feel overloaded and overwhelmed,
   and in being responsible to act to correct it,
      you will be doing the most caring thing possible.

By establishing boundaries about what you're prepared and able to do,
    and when, and where, and how, and why,
        you can help the one you care for, while taking care of yourself.
You'll be able to see more clearly what's happening and what isn't,
    what's needed and what's possible.
You'll come back together with more energy and vitality.
And by creating a separate space for yourself,
    you'll help ensure the one you care for will have *their* own separate space.
They need it as much as you—and perhaps even more.
For they may not have the strength or clarity to create that space on their own.
Once you have established clear boundaries,
    you can approach one another with a freedom and an honesty,
        with an objectivity and a directness, that would not otherwise happen.
And you will be the closer for having stayed apart.

Love consists in this:
that two solitudes protect and border and salute each other.
RAINER MARIA RILKE

Good fences make good neighbors.
ROBERT FROST

It is love that asks,
that seeks,
that knocks,
that finds,
and that is faithful in what it finds.
ST. AUGUSTINE

SUGGESTIONS

Create a "time out" sign and use it.
Everyone needs "time out" periods. Sometimes you won't feel like talking or being bothered. You will crave a few moments to yourself, free of demands and obligations. Find a way to communicate that need in a visible, friendly manner. Wear a certain hat or apron, or tuck something in your shirt pocket so the other person will know. Encourage the one in your care to create a similar "time out" sign, perhaps by turning on a light by the bed, or draping a towel over the bedpost. Being able to create these islands of quiet time without offending the other person can be a lifesaver.

Define your limits.
Everyone has things they cannot or should not do in their caregiving. What are yours? How much should you lift? How long can you stay awake? How do you feel about cooking? How cheerful can you be before your morning coffee? Be clear about what you're able and willing to do. Be just as clear about what you will not do. If it's appropriate, let the one in your care know your limits. Learn to say "no" when it's important to do so. Give thought to how you can honor your limits while seeing that the other person is adequately cared for. Trust others to assist you. Ask for help.

Create your own space.
Carve out an area that is uniquely yours. This might be in the same room where you do most of your caregiving or another room. Design it to suit your tastes. Include whatever feels comfortable and homey to you: pictures, a favorite chair, a desk, writing supplies, books and magazines, family mementos, something from nature. What about treating yourself to something special—a music system, a new piece of artwork, a beverage warmer? Caring for your surroundings can be an important way of caring for yourself.

In accepting your helplessness, you become a better helper.

One reason you're a caregiver is you believe you can make a difference.

You want to play a role in correcting what has gone awry, if that's possible.

You want to assure and comfort.

In a word, you want to help.

There is a difficult double lesson that any caregiver must learn.

One lesson is, no matter how much you do to help,

    there is still much you cannot do.

The other's pain cannot be absorbed or taken away.

The other's mending can be neither hurried nor circumvented.

And if they must accept these things, so must you.

Sometimes the other's condition will not improve, no matter what you do.

Sometimes what you have to offer is rejected,

    and you are powerless to give what you have to give.

The more you come to know what your caregiving can accomplish,

    the more you also come to know what it cannot accomplish.

Another difficult lesson you must learn is this:

however much care you *can* provide,

it may not be the amount of care, or the kind of care, you *should* provide.

Caregivers sometimes try to do too much.

Out of your own needs,

or out of your own unknowing,

you may try to do what someone else is better placed to do.

Perhaps there is another who needs or deserves to be by that person's side,

in addition to you, or instead of you.

Just as importantly, perhaps the "someone" who needs to do more

is the one you are caring for.

It may be that she or he would benefit from having less done rather than more,

for their own strength or self-esteem or integrity.

There is a price that goes with being too dependent.

As you come to understand and accept the ways you cannot and should not help,

you open opportunities for genuine caregiving to happen.

You permit yourself to do what is uniquely yours to do:

to be really with the person you're caring for,

side by side, heart to heart.

You free yourself to help create an environment

in which healing can begin to take place on its own,

whether that healing is physical, emotional, or spiritual—or all of these.

By acknowledging there is much beyond your ability and control,

you make room for the unfolding of that healing potential

which is miraculously built into every human being.

You help shape that sacred space in which people can meet on the deepest level,

where relationships can be redeemed, and love can be rekindled.

In other words, you can move out of the way

and allow the Source of All Life to be the source of all life.

As you do so, you fulfill your calling as a caring helper.

Our letting go is in order that God might be God in us.
MEISTER ECKHART

When other helpers fail and comforts flee,
Help of the helpless, oh, abide with me.
HENRY FRANCIS LYTE

God is our refuge and strength, a very present help in trouble.
Therefore we will not fear, though the earth should change,
though the mountains shake in the heart of the sea.
PSALM 46:1-2

God comes in where my helplessness begins.
OSWALD CHAMBERS

SUGGESTIONS

Inspect your feelings of helplessness.
No one likes to feel powerless. But it's possible to learn valuable information about yourself by examining the way you respond to such feelings. What are times of helplessness like for you? What usually provokes them? What other feelings emerge at such times? Can you recall similar experiences early in your life that made you feel powerless and helpless? What people or settings come to mind? How have you gotten through such times in the past? How might you take better advantage of prayer and meditation during these periods? How could feelings of powerlessness enrich your understanding and experience of trust in God?

Learn how others have coped with powerlessness.
Both you and the one in your care probably have similar feelings of powerlessness, though for different reasons. You can benefit from reading about others' experiences with such feelings. Dale Larson's *The Helper's Journey: Working with People Facing Grief, Loss, and Life-Threatening Illness* contains specific advice. Wendy Lustbader's *Counting on Kindness: An Exploration of Dependency* helps explain what it's like for care receivers. Other helpful books for caregivers are Maggie Strong's *Mainstay: For the Spouse of the Chronically Ill*, Harry Cole's *Helpmates: Support in Times of Critical Illness*, and *Witness to Illness: Strategies for Caregiving and Coping* by Karen Horowitz and Douglas Lanes.

Communicate with the one in your care.
If your situation calls for it and your partner in care is open to it, talk about the idea that caregivers sometimes try to do too much. Ask them if this applies to you. Listen carefully and non-defensively if they answer affirmatively. Learn about specific incidents that serve as examples. Talk about a related idea: sometimes care receivers would benefit from doing more on their own. Ask if that is true for them. Discuss ways you can both work to improve the situation.

Caregiving is more than giving care. It's also receiving care.

Whether your caring is for someone who's long been a part of your life,
   or for someone who is the recipient of the work you've chosen,
      chances are you first assumed your role with a particular idea in mind.
Someone needed care, you thought,
   and you had care to give.
Then you gave,
   and the other received.
While a warm, caregiving relationship may begin that way,
   it seldom ends that way.
True caregiving seldom goes in only one direction.

When you give from the depths of who you are,
you do more than just give—you also gain.
When you truly reach out to another,
something comes back to you.
As for that person who receives your care—
when they sense they're treated with respect and compassion,
when they're valued for what *they* have to offer,
they do much more than just receive.
They give as well.
They may give you their moral support, or gentle guidance,
or quiet understanding.
They may offer you their wisdom, or cheer, or gratitude, or honesty.
They may bestow on you their courage, their hope, their faith.
In short, they may, in their own way and in their own time,
be a caregiver no less than you.

At its best, caregiving is more like *care sharing*.

It's a partnering that develops.

The two of you give, and you find yourselves given to.

The two of you receive, and what you each receive is different,

and it's what you each need.

Both of you are linked together,

and an energy flows back and forth and back again.

There are times in that process

when caregiving and care receiving fall away altogether.

When that happens, what remains is only you as people:

two human beings who care for one another,

who hope for one another,

and who give thanks for one another.

And then caregiving becomes not a duty you do, but a grace you receive.

And care receiving becomes not a gift you passively accept,

but a contribution you actively make.

There are two ways of spreading light:
to be the candle
or the mirror that reflects it.
EDITH WHARTON

Those whom we support hold us up in life.
ANNE SOPHIE SWETCHINE

Blessed are those who can give without remembering,
and take without forgetting.
ELIZABETH BIBESCOE

What we love we shall grow to resemble.
BERNARD OF CLAIRVAUX

SUGGESTIONS

Start a notebook to record the gifts you receive from caregiving.
Purchase a small notebook and keep it handy for jotting down reflections. Write about the experiences in caregiving that bring you joy or contentment or meaning. When you make a discovery, write it down. When the one in your care helps you or educates you or inspires you, write about it. Watch for such gifts and note each one—no matter how small. Keep your notebook in one place in the room and let your partner in care know they're welcome to read from it. Or read aloud from your notes and talk together about the gifts you have received. Be honest—people know when you're only buttering them up—but do be alert to the experiences of grace that come your way.

Give your partner in care a thank-you gift.
Wrap up something meaningful for him or her. It needn't be a big gift—in fact, it *shouldn't* be. It might be something you make, or something of your own you give away. Just make sure it's something you feel the other would like. Be clear why you're offering the present. It is a token of your gratitude for what this person has added to your life.

Allow others to care for you.
Sometimes the care you receive comes not from your care partner but from others around you: family members, friends, neighbors, your clergyperson, other health-care workers. The most important thing you can do for those people—and for yourself—is to accept their care willingly, gratefully, and quietly. Remember that the care you accept is also a validation of this "care sharing" principle. Bask in their concern and affection. Enjoy their tribute. They will profit as much as you.

As a caregiver, your strength is in your flexibility.

To be strong, it is often thought, is to remain firm.

To lead, it is often thought, is to have all the answers.

But genuine caregiving follows another set of rules.

Sometimes one must unlearn what seems right

    so one can relearn what works best.

And often what works best in caregiving

    has nothing to do with being strong in the traditional sense.

Caregiving is not about being uncompromisingly rigid,

    nor is it about knowing all the answers.

Often what works best in caregiving is just the opposite:

    a willingness to be unsure,

        a readiness to bend.

Often what works well is approaching your role with a beginner's mind,

    so you're always exploring, always learning.

What will help both caregiver and care receiver is an elasticity,

    so you can give and bend, without breaking.

Everyone is unique.

You certainly are.

The person you care for undoubtedly is.

So is every family setting and every caregiving situation.

Therefore your task as an effective caregiver

is to respond to the uniqueness of the person you're paired with

and the situation with which you're both confronted.

This will mean you'll probably do better with fewer rather than more rules.

You'll both benefit from less emphasis on "right ways" and "wrong ways,"

and more emphasis on understanding ways and loving ways.

Caregiving is not a time to try to be flawless.

It's a time to be flowing.

It's a time to express your strength through gentleness,

a time to be tender in your touch and in your talk,

a time to be sensitive in your interactions and expectations.

Almost a thousand years ago, a Tibetan named Milarepa
spoke words that every caregiver would do well to take to heart.
"Hasten slowly," he said, "that you may soon arrive."
Hasten slowly, as caregivers and care receivers,
that you may reach the destination you each seek,
and in the manner you each deserve.
Hasten slowly, and learn the practice of patience—
patience with the person you care for,
and patience with yourself.
Hasten slowly, and learn the art of forgiving,
as you look into one another's eyes,
and as you see your own face reflected there.
Hasten slowly, and learn the discipline of being sturdy enough to bend,
and firm enough to yield.
As you do so, your caregiving will assume strength
it would not otherwise have.

If you stop to be kind, you must swerve often from your path.
MARY WEBB

Don't grit your teeth and clench your fists
and say "I will! I will!"
Relax. Take your hands off. Submit yourself to God.
Learn to live in the passive voice . . .
and let life be willed through you.
THOMAS KELLY

Be ever soft and pliable like a reed,
not hard and unbending like a cedar.
THE TALMUD

You learn through mistakes—no one was born a master.
SWISS PROVERB

SUGGESTIONS

Develop contingency plans.
Sometimes things will not go as you wish. You will become ill, or something unexpected will happen to the one in your care. Unforeseen events will disrupt your carefully made plans and routines. When this happens, you'll need new strategies. Make sure you've thought through options ahead of time. Have in mind people you can turn to. Check with them in advance to confirm their interest and availability. Create backup plans, and make sure someone else knows about them, too.

Learn how to brainstorm.
When you face a dilemma or difficulty in caregiving, you will have more ways of responding than you may initially realize. Brainstorming can help you expand the possibilities. Start by listing options that easily come to mind. Write them down so you can see and remember them. Add as many more as you can—ideas that seem funny or weird count, too. Involve others in the process: your care partner, friends, medical staff. Build on one another's creativity and originality. Check what others have done in similar situations. When you've exhausted your ideas, go back through the list, eliminating what won't work, prioritizing what might work, and choosing what will work best. Keep an open mind. Have fun with the exercise.

Purposefully change your routine.
Avoid always doing your tasks at the very same time and in the very same way. Shake things up sometimes. For instance, reverse the order in which you perform certain duties, if the order isn't important. Intentionally change the way you begin or end a task or activity. Add a read-aloud hour. Take a fresh-air break. Look for ways to add freshness and spontaneity to your roles and relationships. That way you'll help to minimize effects of unplanned and *necessary* changes in the future. You'll be a veteran at flexibility long before you're called to be.

The only way to support another effectively is to be effectively supported.

However strong you are as a caregiver, your strength will run out.

For you cannot perform indefinitely without support.

No one can.

However much patience and kindness you possess, you have limits.

Everyone does.

And even though you may know a great deal about caring for that other person, you don't know enough.

You *can't* know enough.

This is not a matter of your memory or intelligence.

It has nothing to do with your motivation or devotion.

It has to do with your involvement and your perspective.

Some things are difficult to see when you're too close.

Some things are hard to sort out when you're entangled with so many details.

Some decisions are too far-reaching to make without outside input.

You need help.

You would not want the one you're caring for to go without help.

Similarly, you dare not wish anything less for yourself.

You need your own opportunities to be nurtured and nourished.

You need your own freedom to vent your feelings
   without fear you'll offend the other.

You need the chance to learn how others have done what is now yours to do.

You deserve to be around someone who will validate you,
   someone who is interested, someone who will care.

If you're part of a team of caregivers,
   you can turn to other team members and ask for what you need.

You can open yourself to their viewpoint and insight.

If you're more alone in your role,
   you can join a caregivers' support group in your community.

You might speak with a medical professional or mental health specialist,
   a chaplain or a clergyperson.

You might create your own caregiving team:
   family and friends, neighbors and colleagues—anyone you trust.

Once your support system is in place, take advantage of it.

Accept graciously others' offers of assistance.

Learn to ask for what you need.

Make sure you have time off and time away,

and treat this time not as a luxury, but as what it is: a human necessity.

Listen to those who are more experienced and borrow their ideas.

Find at least one person with whom you can really be yourself.

Figure out which people you can call upon at various times—

when you need to sound off, or when you could use a good laugh;

when you need a strong shoulder, or when you could use a pep talk.

Remember, too, that support is available on another plane.

You'll find that God is always present,

offering you hope when your own is in short supply,

lending you assurance when you wonder how you'll survive.

We want people to feel with us more than to act for us.
GEORGE ELIOT

Listen to advice and accept instruction,
that you may gain wisdom for the future.
PROVERBS 19:20

You alone can do it, but you cannot do it alone.
O. HOBART MOWRER

The delicate and infirm go for sympathy,
not to the well and buoyant,
but to those who have suffered like themselves.
CATHARINE ESTHER BEECHER

SUGGESTIONS

Join or start a caregiver support group.
If you're the primary caregiver for a family member or friend, you'll benefit from talking honestly with people in similar situations. That's the kind of atmosphere a support group can provide. You have unique stresses, conflicting emotions, and unusual demands that need to be discussed and shared. A support group can give you strength to keep going. Check with your local mental health center to see if an appropriate group meets in your area. Or call a hospital's social services department, a nearby hospice, or a 24-hour community help line. If an appropriate support group isn't available and you have the energy, consider starting one. If you're a professional caregiver, try meeting with colleagues to talk about how you deal with your roles.

Join or start a caregiver co-op.
Sharing caregiving tasks with people in similar situations is a wonderful way to help and be helped. Share rides to doctor appointments or therapy sessions. Shop for one another or pick up prescriptions and medical supplies on a rotating basis. Stand in for one another so each caregiver has time to handle other responsibilities or simply to get away for a bit. Cook for one another or eat together if you wish. Offer to trade services, doing what you're good at in exchange for a skill you're lacking.

Locate support on the computer Internet.
If your caregiving duties keep you tied down, you can find support without leaving your chair. You'll need access to a computer, hookup to the Internet, and a little time to learn your way around. (If necessary, enlist the help of a friend or neighbor.) You can communicate one-on-one or in small groups with fellow caregivers across town or around the world. You can ask questions of professionals. You can tap into vast amounts of information free of charge: caregiving tips, facts about diseases and disabilities, access to organizations, and lots more.

In the ordinariness of your caregiving lies something more: sacredness.

You have already learned this:

much about caregiving revolves around the ordinary.

You have everyday routines to follow,

predictable tasks to perform,

mundane details to attend to.

Your caregiving often occurs in settings that are commonplace,

among ordinary people who do ordinary things in ordinary ways.

Yet deep within all that is ordinary about your caregiving and care receiving

lies the possibility of contact with what you might not expect:

a sense of the sacred.

This serendipity can happen in various ways.

53

As you engage in simple acts of care,
   you may begin to witness signs of the Divine in your midst.
It can be seen in one another's face.
It can be felt in one another's touch.
It can be heard in one another's voice.
As you share with one another the common stories of your lives,
   you can begin to see themes that are eternal and threads of the everlasting.
As you draw closer to one another in the partnership of your care,
   you can find that you draw closer to that Someone who is beyond yourselves,
      and ever so near.
The caregiving ritual can take on a spiritual dimension in another way.

By being very present in each act of care,
   by being very conscious of the passing moments you share,
      you can experience what people of faith and wisdom have taught for ages.
The here and the now is not just here and now.
Yes, it is that; but it is also much more.

By taking the time not just to look, but to really see,

    not just to listen, but to truly hear,

        not just to touch, but to be healing in that touch,

            your moments of caregiving become more than mere moments.

They become times on earth that are infused with a bit of heaven.

They become experiences that ground you in living and root you in meaning.

They become reminders that while you're sharing in caregiving,

    others are engaged in similar acts elsewhere and everywhere.

Together you are participating in the grand dance of life

    with all the generations who have gone before you,

        and with all who will ever follow you.

And you recognize that it is not just you who act.

It is not just you who give care and receive care.

A Presence acts through you, and in you, and even apart from you.

And yours is the privilege to witness that miracle.

Have thy heart in heaven and thy hands upon the earth.
Ascend in piety and descend in charity.
For this is the Nature of Light and the way of the children of it.

THOMAS VAUGHAN

Love seeketh not itself to please,
Nor for itself hath any care,
But for another gives its ease,
And builds a Heaven in hell's despair.

WILLIAM BLAKE

To be really great in little things,
to be truly noble and heroic in the insipid details of everyday life,
is a virtue so rare as to be worthy of canonization.

HARRIET BEECHER STOWE

It is only by forgetting yourself that you draw near to God.

HENRY DAVID THOREAU

SUGGESTIONS

Begin each day with quiet time and prayer.
Start your day by centering yourself. Take at least twenty minutes to meet your spiritual needs and prepare for your day. Read passages of scripture and meditate on the words. Read religious writings that nurture your soul: books, articles, sermons, prayers, poems, hymns. Listen to sacred music, or sing it, or play it. Sit in silence, listening for God's voice. Pray. Pray for the one in your care, for yourself as a caregiver, for others. Carry this time with you throughout the day.

Treat your caregiving as sacred.
Remember the words of St. Benedict, a fifth-century Christian: "Treat all your tools and instruments as though they were sacred vessels of the altar." Follow his advice. Treat all your instruments, aids, and supplies as if they were sacred. Ask God's blessing on your use of them, then use them thoughtfully, gently, reverently. Approach your partner in care as a sacred gift from God. View your caregiving routines as rituals as well as chores.

Dedicate each day to God.
In your time of prayer and meditation, choose one specific principle which will be the theme for your day. For example, "love," "patience," "hope," "gentleness." Take a single line from scripture and repeat it to yourself throughout the day, reflecting on its meaning for the various moods and situations that arise.

Create a sacred space.
Somewhere in the room where you regularly work, place signs of things that carry spiritual significance for you: a painting or photograph or poster, a Bible or cross or religious emblem. Put a candle or incense nearby and burn it at certain times. Ask the person in your care what they would like, and be sensitive to their desires.

The Grace of Being a Caregiver

Every caregiver experiences a call.

For some, that call comes in the anxious voice of a family member or friend,

   or with an imploring look in their eyes,

      either of which says, "I need you."

For some, the call comes through anonymous faces lined with suffering,

   both young and old, both near and far.

For some, the call is handed from one generation to another, like a trust;

   or from guide to pilgrim, like an honor;

      or from lover to loved, like a gift.

For some, the call is carried by that Voice from above, that Spirit at their side.

However it comes, the communication is the same:

   "You are wanted."

However it's delivered, the question is implicit:

   "Will you help?"

It's not easy being a caregiver.
There are days when your vitality runs low,
   when your spirit sags,
      when your anxiety peaks.
There are times when the hours are too long,
   when the demands seem too many,
      when the rewards feel too few.
There may be instances when the other is hard to care for—
   they may be angry or depressed and take it out on you;
      they may feel lost or forsaken and push away your efforts to help.
There may be periods when you feel unacknowledged or unappreciated,
   when you feel lonely and alone.
There may be times when what's expected of you seems beyond your abilities,
   when what's asked of you is more than you have to give.
Being a caregiver has demands and difficulties,
   annoyances and adversities.
It has its full share of pain.

Yet being a caregiver can be one of the most meaningful things you'll ever do.
You can help a fellow human being as you yourself would want to be helped.
You can do for another what they could not do without you.
You may be able to nurse them back to health and vitality,
　　or you may accompany them to a place of relative calm and stability,
　　　　or you may witness their journey from life on earth to a life beyond.
But that is only the beginning.
There will be times in your caregiving when you realize,
　　however much the other has gained,
　　　　you have gained just as much, and perhaps even more.
In the act of accepting, you will be accepted in a way you have not before.
In the act of comforting, you will be unexpectedly comforted.
In the act of dying with another, you will be reborn.
There will be times in your caregiving when,
　　however tired you are, you're ever so alive;
　　　　however separate you feel, you're ever so connected;
　　　　　　whatever brokenness you've known, you've never felt more whole.
Those will be the times when you begin to fathom what it means to love.

Through the discipline of your caregiving,
   you will experience marvelous new awareness.
In being a blessing for another, you are blessed.
In being a vehicle for growth, you grow.
In being a conduit for healing, you are healed.
And, in holding out the promise that, no matter what has happened,
   transformation is still possible, then you yourself can be transformed.
Caregiver and care receiver alike transform one another.
One of you loves, and one of you is loved, and you're both the same.
And you will know that transformation is not something *you* have accomplished.
It comes from beyond you.

You will realize, if you do not already,
   that you are cared for on the grandest scale possible.
And the most fitting response you can make is a prayer
   that contains only four words:
      Thank you.
      Thank you.

THE CAREGIVER'S BOOK
Caring for Another, Caring for Yourself

Text design by Melanie Lawson

Scripture quotations are from the New Revised Standard Version Bible, copyright © 1989 by the Division of Christian Education of the National Council of the Churches of Christ in the U.S.A. and used by permission, and from the Revised Standard Version of the Bible, copyright © 1946, 1952, 1971 by the Division of Christian Education of the National Council of the Churches of Christ in the U.S.A. and used by permission.

Library of Congress Cataloging-in-Publication Data

Miller, James E., 1945-
    The caregiver's book : caring for another, caring for yourself /
text and photography by James E. Miller.
       p. cm. — (The Willowgreen series.)
    Includes bibliographical references.
    ISBN 0-8066-2985-1 (alk. paper)
    1. Caregivers—Religious life. 2. Caring—Religious aspects—
Christianity. I. Title. II. Series: Miller, James E., 1945-
Willowgreen series.
BV4910.9.M55 1996
248.8'9—dc20

96-23938
CIP